CRYPTOCURRENCY
HOW TO PROFIT FROM FREE LABOR

KAKRA BAIDEN

Copyright © 2019 by Airpower Publishing, LLC

Cryptocurrency
How to Profit from Free Labor
by Kakra Baiden

Printed in the United States of America

ISBN: 978-1-945123-17-7

All rights reserved. No part of this document may be reproduced or transmitted in any form, by any means (electronic, photocopying, recording, or otherwise) without the written permission of the author.

Unless otherwise indicated, Bible quotations are taken from New International Version – UK (NIVUK) Holy Bible, New International Version® Anglicized, NIV® Copyright © 1979, 1984, 2011 by Biblica, Inc.® Used by permission. All rights reserved worldwide.

Scripture marked KJV is taken from the King James Version of the Bible. Public domain.

Scripture marked NKJV is taken from the New King James Version® of the Bible. Copyright © 1982 by Thomas Nelson. Used by permission. All rights reserved.

Dedication

Dedicated to Ebo Assan
Thanks for the input you have made in my life.

Table of Contents

Chapter 1
    There Is Profit in All Labor 7

Chapter 2
    The Definition of Profit..11

Chapter 3
    Profit Has to Be Identified..................................23

Chapter 4
    What to Do after Identifying Your "Profit" 45

Chapter 5
    How You Can Profit from Serving the Lord....55

Chapter 6
    Conditions for Serving God................................67

About the Author Kakra Baiden.............................71

Chapter 1

There Is Profit in All Labor

Cryptocurrency

RECENTLY SOMEONE CAME to my office and tried to convince me to invest in cryptocurrency.

Money evolves and has been evolving throughout human history. From gold coins, to paper money, to digital money, to cryptocurrency. Cryptocurrency is derived from the Greek word *cryptography*. *Crypto* means hidden or secret, and *graphy* means writing. Cryptocurrency is a digital currency that operates outside a central bank and is protected and regulated by its security features.

Spiritual Cryptocurrency

Today I want to introduce you to what I call a "spiritual cryptocurrency." Let's examine the term in detail. It's spiritual because the concept is taken from the Bible, so it's based on spiritual principles. Why do I call it a cryptocurrency? I will break down the word so you understand me more clearly.

The word *crypto* is originally a Greek word that means something that is hidden. What I am about to share with you has a hidden value that's hidden from the normal eye. It's normally not considered as money, but you can reap huge profits from it.

Graphy means a writing that has a hidden meaning. It's "graphy" because it's written in hidden spiritual code: the Word of God. Scripture states, "The person without the Spirit does not accept the things that come from the Spirit of God but considers them foolishness, and cannot understand them because they are discerned only through the Spirit" (1 Corinthians 2:14).

Finally, you can profit from it because it's a "currency"; it can be used as a medium of exchange for goods and services. You may ask, "What currency is this?" It's called free labor. You can profit from free labor. "In all labour there is profit: but the talk of the lips tendeth only to penury" (Proverbs 14:23, KJV).

The Word of God states that there is profit to be made in all labor, both paid and unpaid. It's easy to accept that there is profit in paid labor, but in unpaid labor! That sounds ridiculous. But that's exactly my point. Free labor can act as a currency and bring you great profit. Are you ready to make huge profits from this cryptocurrency called free labor? Then keep on reading reading.

My Pastor's House

Years ago, my pastor, Dag Heward-Mills, asked me to help him build his house. I was in my teens and a student of architecture. He introduced me to his contractor, Mr. Annan, and asked me to assist him.

I used to wake up around five a.m., get ready, and report at the site. I started at six a.m. and closed around six p.m. each day. The contractor made me do procurement, plus many other jobs he assigned to me. By the time I finally got home I would be very tired, and the cycle would repeat itself. I worked hard and long for free, but I was happy to help my pastor. Although I wasn't paid physically, I profited in many ways from rendering my services for free, and I continue to reap profits from that experience.

Are you interested in making huge profits? The good news is you can, whether you are paid or not paid for your services. Keep on reading and get ready to make unimaginable profits above your pay grade. Your earnings will multiply and it will impact every area of your life: spiritual, mental, physical, emotional, financial, marital, you name it. I am talking about a comprehensive blessing. You may ask, "How can I do this?" By working for free.

The Scripture states that "in all labor there is profit." This means there is profit in both unpaid and paid work. It's better to work for someone for free at your own expense than to sit at home unemployed.

You may be thinking, *Is this possible? How can you make profit by working for free? Who pays you at the end?* Let me show you how you can do this. It begins with a mental shift. First of all, you must change your definition of profit.

Chapter 2

The Definition of Profit

What Does It Mean to Make Profit?

WHEN WE TALK about profit, most people's minds gravitate towards money; dollars. They begin to see green everywhere. If you have that mind-set, you cannot profit from free labor. The definition of profit should not be held captive by the narrow cell of finances. Until you change your definition of profit, you cannot recognize other forms of "crypto," or hidden profit.

This is crucial, because the way you think about something determines your response. "For as he thinketh in his heart, so is he" (Proverbs 23:7, KJV). Transformation comes from changing your mind. "Do not conform to the pattern of this world, but be transformed by the renewing of your mind" (Romans 12:2).

Let's examine some definitions of profit.

1. The Definition of Profit: Profit Means to Get Gain

It was dawn and the tired fisherman who had been fishing unsuccessfully all night was washing his net after a hard day's work. He started the day with hopes of making profit, but now he was facing heavy losses. The fishes had outsmarted and eluded him.

It can be very frustrating when you put in a lot and have very little return on your investments. It could be an investment in love that yielded no marriage; an investment in a job which finally led to a dismissal; or an investment in in an exam which ended in failure. But this was a failed financial investment. Remember, God is in the miracle business.

Suddenly the fisherman saw a young man in his early thirties with a crowd in tow approaching him. The young man stepped into his boat without his consent, which was beached nearby, and audaciously asked him if he could use his services and his boat for free.

I can imagine the mixed emotions of anger, incredulity, and confusion that may have rocked his head, but he acquiesced. He left his net and agreed to work for free for this stranger whom he had just met.

Some in the crowd may have thought, What a big fool, he should have charged him. How was he going to provide for his wife kids and pay his mortgage?

The young man introduced himself as Jesus of Nazareth, the carpenter's son, and he introduced himself as Simon Peter, the fisherman. Peter agreed to work for Jesus for free. This is the biblical account of this incident.

"One day as Jesus was standing by the Lake of Gennesaret, the people were crowding around him and listening to the word of God. He saw at the water's edge two boats, left there by the fishermen, who were washing their nets. He got into one of the boats, the one belonging to Simon, and asked him to put out a little from shore. Then he sat down and taught the people from the boat.

When he had finished speaking, he said to Simon, "Put out into deep water, and let down the nets for a catch."

Simon answered, "Master, we've worked hard all night and haven't caught anything. But because you say so, I will let down the nets."

When they had done so, they caught such a large number of fish that their nets began to break. So they signaled their partners in the other boat to come and help them, and they came and filled both boats so full that they began to sink.

When Simon Peter saw this, he fell at Jesus' knees and said, "Go away from me, Lord; I am a sinful man!" (Luke 5:1-8).

The "Profit" of God's Word

Peter did not gain money, but one of the things he gained was the Word of God. He sat down and listened to Jesus preach a sermon from his boat.

Imagine if Peter had refused to work for free and demanded money for his services. We would not be talking about him today. Peter became a beneficiary of God's Word.

I want us to examine some of the potential blessings he may have gained from God's Word. These are the words of David concerning the potential blessings of God's Word.

> "The law of the Lord is perfect,
>   converting the soul:
> the testimony of the Lord is sure,
>   making wise the simple.
> The statutes of the Lord are right,
>   rejoicing the heart:
> the commandment of the Lord is pure,
>   enlightening the eyes.
> The fear of the Lord is clean, enduring for ever:
> the judgments of the Lord are true and
>   righteous altogether.
> More to be desired are they than gold, yea,
>   than much fine gold:
> sweeter also than honey and the honeycomb.
> Moreover by them is thy servant warned:
> and in keeping of them there is great reward"
> (Psalm 19:7-11, NKJV).

These marvelous blessings cannot be compared to the money Jesus would have paid Peter. How much would it have been?

Let's Examine Some of These Gains in Detail

The Word of God is profitable and diverse in its nature. It affects every area of your life: spirit, soul, and body. You can profit from it in several ways.

Conversion
"The law of the LORD is perfect converting the soul."

This encounter was the genesis of Peter's conversion from a fisherman to an apostle. I became converted when a young pastor at that time. Dag Heward-Mills came to my house and spoke to me about giving my life to Jesus. I did, and God's Word converted me from a sinner into a man of God, a good husband, and a responsible father.

Wisdom
"The testimony of the LORD is sure,
making wise the simple."

Just yesterday I was speaking to a young man and I advised him to marry early because it's a wise decision. The Bible says rejoice with the wife of your youth (Proverbs 5:19). He asked me why. I went on to explain that it brings focus into your life. It helps you focus your time, energy, resources, and emotions. If not, these resources can be dissipated on causal relationships and adventures.

God's Word makes us wise.

After the sermon, Peter made the wise decision to follow Jesus. That's the smartest decision an individual can make. "He left all and followed him."

Joy
*"The statutes of the L*ORD *are right, rejoicing the heart."*

One day a man who was tired of life and ready to end his life heard me preaching. Joy was rekindled in his heart and the energy to continue living returned. He aborted his suicide mission. God's Word can bring joy into your heart.

Imagine how depressed Peter might have been after toiling all night and ending up with nothing. I am sure the Word encouraged him. Joy is a source of energy.

When you lose your joy in marriage, business, ministry, or relationship with God, you will find it difficult to continue because of a lack of energy. That's why we are to "run with perseverance the race marked out for us, fixing our eyes on Jesus, the pioneer and perfecter of faith. For the joy set before him he endured the cross" (Hebrews 12:1-2).

Jesus found energy to finish His race because of inner joy, and so will you.

After the preaching, Peter found energy to go fishing again. Are you tired? Read the Word. It gives energy.

Guidance
*"The commandment of the L*ORD *is pure, enlightening the eyes."*

To enlighten means to throw light on something. Light makes the eyes to see and reveals the true nature of things. The light of God's Word is a lamp unto our feet and a light unto our path; it guides us.

I once came across a man who had not spoken to his dad for sixteen years; he was being guided by bitterness. After the sermon, he cried bitterly and told me he had repented. That very night he called his dad and reconciled with him. The Word started guiding him in his relationships.

Peter was guided by Jesus' words to try again and not to throw in the towel. He had been fishing unsuccessfully all night. He tried again, and this time he succeeded.

Holiness
"The fear of the LORD *is clean, enduring forever."*

Sometime back a friend of mine introduced me to a certain quiet, shy-looking gentleman. Later on he told me that same quiet gentleman had killed several people. Suddenly I began to fear him, based on what I now knew about him. I became careful of what I did or said, so as not to provoke him in any way, lest I become his next victim. I began to fear him when I got to know more about him.

Some people don't fear God because they don't know much about Him. The more you know Him, the more you will fear Him. The Word reveals who God is, and this knowledge helps us to be holy because we become aware that although God is loving, "our God is a consuming fire" (Hebrews 12:29).

After the encounter with Jesus, Peter became afraid of Jesus and realized he was a sinful man. He said, "depart from me, for I am a sinful man." Holiness makes you disciplined, and discipline is a key for success in every area.

Truth
"The judgments of the LORD *are true and righteous."*

In reality, Peter was a failed fisherman, at least for that day, but when Jesus sat in his boat He revealed to him truth from God's Word. He said, "Let down your net for a catch." He changed his truth.

As you get older you begin to realize more and more that God's Word is true. You will see prophecy literally being fulfilled in people's lives for good or for bad.

I agree with Job, who said, "We have examined this, and it is true. So hear it and apply it to yourself" (Job 5:27).

If you don't walk in truth, you will walk in deception. "His word is truth" (John 17:17).

Warnings
"By them is your servant warned."

For example, the Word warns us that there is life after death, and after that, judgment. We must prepare to meet our Maker.

Do you think these blessings can be substituted for a few "dollars?" By working free for Jesus, Peter was saved from eternal damnation. The words of Jesus warned him.

2. The Definition of Profit: Profit Means to Get an Advantage

I once travelled with a friend of mine to another country. We both purchased economy tickets for the journey. As we made our way to the gate, he said, "We will converse more when we get on the plane."

I said, "We will not be sitting together because I will be upgraded to business." He asked me how that was going to be possible, and I told him the anointing or power of God would give me an advantage.

True to my word, I was ushered into the business class section when we boarded. He was sent to economy. Later I teased him that a screen was pulled, so I didn't endure seeing his face.

An advantage is something that puts you in a better position than others. Peter had an advantage over his fellow struggling fishermen. Jesus had decided to go fishing with him. He did not gain money, but he gained the anointing or power of God. The miracle-working power of God made him catch fish he had never caught before. Their boats even sunk from the weight of the fish. He was so blessed he became afraid.

May God bless you with a job, spouse, house, car, etc., that will make you afraid. This was Peter's response to his bumper catch: "When Simon Peter saw this, he fell at Jesus' knees and said, 'Go away from me, Lord; I am a sinful man!' For he and all his companions were astonished at the catch of fish they had taken" (Luke 5:8-9).

The fish he caught was more valuable than what he could have charged for his services.

3. The Definition of Profit: Profit Means to Get a Benefit

The benefit of something is the help that you get from it. Relationships can be a source of benefit.

I have met many people in life, great and small, and some of them have been of great benefit to me in diverse ways. God can bring you into relationships that are more beneficial than money. For example, you can benefit from the words and wisdom of others.

Recently I was thinking about my biological dad, and I begin to notice many things I have benefitted from him, especially his wisdom.

Sometimes we can meet people of a lower social and financial stature than us, but they can be a blessing. Sometime back a friend I knew in the past planned to rob me at night, but a young man whom I knew leaked his intentions to me. Maybe on that day he saved my life.

Peter Benefitted from His Relationship with Jesus

Relationships can be more profitable than money because they do not only bring money, but also other things that are unrelated to money.

By working for free, Peter started a relationship with Jesus, and he profited immensely from it. Look at some of the things that happened to him. His confidence and IQ went up by association: "When they saw the courage of Peter and John and realized that they were unschooled, ordinary men, they were astonished and they took note that these men had been with Jesus" (Acts 4:13).

He became an anointed and prosperous man: "With great power the apostles continued to testify to the resurrection of the Lord Jesus. And God's grace was so powerfully at work in them all that there were no needy persons among them. For from time to time those who owned land or houses sold them, brought the money from the sales and put it at the apostles' feet, and it was distributed to anyone who had need" (Acts 4:33-35).

Through him many were saved and healed by his ministry: "Nevertheless, more and more men and women believed in the Lord and were added to their number. As a result, people brought the sick into the streets and laid them on beds and mats so that at least Peter's shadow might fall on some of them as he passed by" (Acts 5:14-15).

How much money can be compared to this? In all labor there is profit.

The Story of Cara Wood

In 1992, Cara Wood was seventeen and working at Drin's Colonial Restaurant in her hometown of Chagrin Falls, about fifteen miles east of Cleveland, Ohio. She was a good employee—bright, friendly, and helpful. One customer, Bill Cruxton, liked her so much that he always sat in her section. A widower with no children, he went daily to the restaurant for his meals and some company, so they became friends. In addition to being his regular waitress, she helped him around the house and ran errands for him. Wood became so important to Cruxton that he rewrote his will, making her the main beneficiary. Cruxton, 82, died of heart failure in November 1992 and left her half a million dollars.

Relationships can be beneficial, and sometimes the most beneficial relationships have no financial ties. To profit from free labor, you must be able to identify the profit you seek; otherwise you will feel exploited or underpaid.

Chapter 3

Profit Has to Be Identified

IDENTIFY MEANS to know what something is. Until you know what something is, you may not know its value.

How a Great Soccer Player was Identified

The great footballer, Lionel Messi, was discovered by Carles Rexach, former Barcelona player and coach. He was the man who brought Lionel Messi to the attention of the Catalan side. In an interview with *The Sun*, he revealed what he made of the Argentine the first time he saw him play.

"I was in Argentina when they first told me about this lad called Messi," he told *The Sun*. "But I thought they were talking about a boy who was maybe eighteen or twenty. I thought, *Since I'm in Argentina, I'll take a look at him*. But of course, when they told me that the lad was twelve years old, I was a little surprised."

Nevertheless, the youngster was brought over to Spain, and with fears existing over his size, owing to his stunted growth, a friendly game was organised against much bigger, much stronger players in order to give the youngster a true test.

"I got there at five o'clock, and I looked and I walked about a little bit; I looked again," Rexach recalled. "Football is a team game, right? But this kid could play all on his own. He took the ball and beat other players and scored a goal. He had abnormal ability. All instinct. He was born to play football. So when I got back to the bench, I said, 'We have to sign him! That kid is from another galaxy.'"

This scout was able to identify Messi's potential and value before it manifested fully. To profit from free labor, you must be able to identify the profit you seek. Otherwise you will see it as a waste of your time. The profit might differ from person to person, based on each person's expectation.

Paul Identified Onesimus

In the Bible there is the story of a slave called Onesimus, who ran away from his master, Philemon. Paul later came into contact with him and identified him as a "profitable " person. He wrote a letter to Philemon, his master, pleading with him that the slave he viewed as unprofitable was profitable to him. He said, "I appeal to you for my son Onesimus, who became my son while I was in chains. Formerly he was useless to you, but now he has become useful both to you and to me" (Philemon 1:10-11).

To Philemon, Onesimus was of little economic value, but to Paul he was a great spiritual asset. The profit they sought was different.

Let's examine different types of profit you can make by working for free. When you are able to do this you can work for free wholeheartedly because you have identified what you are working for. Your motivation then becomes your profit—not money.

1. Profit Has to Be Identified: Skill

The Skillful Joiner

Some time ago I came across a skillful joiner who made beautiful, expensive handmade furniture. This man was so good his furniture pieces were simply breathtaking. I wondered where he got his skills from.

I later learnt that he used to be a drug dealer who was arrested and sent to prison. In prison he decided to learn carpentry and offer his services for free. After many years he came out as a master craftsman who had honed his skills by working for free. The skill was his reward, not money, and that skill provided other things, including money. There were reasons why God chose David as king, and these are some of the reasons.

The Example of David

"He chose David his servant and took him from the sheep pens; from tending the sheep he brought him to be the shepherd of his people Jacob, of Israel his inheritance. And David shepherded them with integrity of heart; with skillful hands he led them" (Psalm 78:70-72).

David became king for two reasons: spiritual and natural. First of all, God selected him on the basis of his heart. "The LORD said to Samuel, 'Do not consider his appearance or his height, for I have rejected him. The LORD does not look at the things people look at. People look at the outward appearance, but the LORD looks at the heart' " (1 Samuel 16:7).

Secondly, He chose him because he had the skill of a shepherd. A skill is a job that needs special training or knowledge.

Many times we focus on the spiritual reason why David was chosen, but there was also a natural one. Both are important. What's the use of having an accountant who has integrity but can't keep your books?

You Can Learn a Skill by Working for Free

Where did David get his fighting skills from? As a young boy he used to keep his father's sheep for free. He learnt how to take care of sheep and protect them. You need similar skills to be a shepherd of people. He developed courage and fighting skills by fighting wild animals that sought to catch the sheep.

No wonder when Goliath, the giant, challenged Israel to a one-on-one fight he was unfazed, because he had fought lions and bears. This is David in his own words: "But David said to Saul, 'Your servant has been keeping his father's sheep. When a lion or a bear came and carried off a sheep from the flock, I went after it, struck it and rescued the sheep from its mouth. When it turned on me, I seized it by its hair, struck it and killed it. Your servant has killed both the lion and the bear; this uncircumcised Philistine will be like one of them, because he has defied the armies of the living God. The LORD who rescued me from the paw of the lion and the paw of the bear will rescue me from the hand of this Philistine.' Saul said to David, 'Go, and the LORD be with you' " (1 Samuel 17:34-37).

There is a difference between having a degree and having a skill. You may be unemployed because you lack a skill, not a degree. One easy way to learn a skill is to identify the skill you want and offer your services for free.

Assume you wanted to learn construction. You could volunteer to work for a construction company for free. Through that, vital skills will be passed on to you. Who doesn't want free labor? Many do.

When you even help someone to take care of her baby, you learn the skill of taking care of kids. These skills will become useful when you have your own kids. I have noticed that to be a good businessman, pastor, etc., you need to acquire skills from successful people in your field.

Working for free can bring you into contact with such people and transfer skills and details, which make a big difference. Someone said the devil is in the details, but the angels are also in the details. In all labor there is profit.

2. Profit Has to Be Identified: Favor

Favor Is a Spiritual "Cryptocurrency"

Favor is a currency because it can be used to purchase stuff. The only difference is, it's spiritual in nature.

Favor also commands a higher value than silver and gold. That's why "it is rather to be chosen than silver and gold." "A good name is rather to be chosen than great riches, and loving favour rather than silver and gold" (Proverbs 22:1).

That's why favor is listed as money along with other precious metals, like gold and silver.

Let's look at some aspects of this little-known but powerful currency.

Favor Is "Big Money"

Big money cannot be seen; it's invisible. Billions and trillions are not counted; they move from computer to computer invisibly, wirelessly, and silently.

Small money is usually visible and stored in wallets. That's what we use to buy groceries, etc. That's why favor is invisible.

God has "blessed us in the heavenly realms with every spiritual blessing in Christ" (Ephesians 1:3).

Spiritual blessings are so huge. They are invisible and are stored in our spiritual bank accounts in heaven. They are too big to be carrying around.

What are the things favor can buy?

Favor Can "Buy" Tangible Things

My Conference

I preach the Word of God in over fifty countries through radio and TV. My audience is largely invisible to me, but I spend a huge amount of money on people I don't know. However, as I do this, I seem to build up my "favor account," and sometimes I meet people who bless me for rendering this free service.

One day I decided to hold a conference in one of the countries I broadcast in. It was going to be expensive because I needed to fly my staff, pay hotel bills, rent equipment, etc. Before I arrived, a stranger who had been watching the broadcast provided a car for my use. One afternoon we went to a restaurant for lunch. After lunch we asked for the bill but we were informed another customer had paid our bill and left. He was a complete stranger.

At the end of the conference another stranger came to my hotel room and offered to pay all my bills, including the bills of my staff. By the time I was leaving, everything had been provided and paid for by strangers. I used the cryptocurrency called favor to settle all my bills.

How did I obtain this favor? The broadcast they were watching was a free service provided by me and in that way my "favor account" grew. All these things were paid for with the currency called favor.

Favor and the Children of Israel

The children of Israel were slaves in Egypt for many years. They were not paid for their services, although they labored to build treasure houses for Pharaoh.

What was missing? Favor. One day favor arrived and they became rich overnight. That fateful day, favor bought tangible money: silver and gold. "The Israelites did as Moses instructed and asked the Egyptians for articles of silver and gold and for clothing. The LORD had made the Egyptians favorably disposed toward the people, and they gave them what they asked for; so they plundered the Egyptians" (Exodus 12:35-36).

The Man Who Gave Me a House

I preach on a lot of radio stations in my country. One day a complete stranger who had been blessed by my radio broadcast called me and said, "Pastor, the Lord has asked me to give you a gift."

I answered, "What's it?"

He replied, "A house."

I was dumbfounded and thought he was joking, but he was serious. He later gave me a brand new house. I was so moved I also gave it out as an offering to the Lord. I purchased a brand new house with the spiritual cryptocurrency of favor.

By offering the Gospel for free to the nation on the airwaves, I had increased my "favor account" and was making profit tangibly.

Favor Can "Buy" Intangible Things

Recently I received a call from a distraught and sad father whose son had died in the hospital. He said, choking with tears, "I want you to pray for my son."

I asked, "What's the problem?"

He responded, "He is dead." For some seconds the phone went dead as I ruminated on this sad message. He said with a croaking voice, "I want you to pray for him so God will raise him from the dead."

This man believed I had more favor with God so God would answer my prayer more than his. I prayed with him, and after about five minutes he called me again, this time with joy and excitement in his voice. God had resurrected his son! The boy came back to life. That's the power of favor with God.

Favor is an invisible currency that can be traded in the spiritual and natural realm.

How a Family Profited from Favor with Jesus

"Now a man named Lazarus was sick. He was from Bethany, the village of Mary and her sister

Martha. (This Mary, whose brother Lazarus now lay sick, was the same one who poured perfume on the Lord and wiped his feet with her hair.) So the sisters sent word to Jesus, 'Lord, the one you love is sick' " (John 11:1-3).

Martha and Mary had noticed Jesus had powerful prayers with tangible results. Earlier He had turned water into wine at a wedding. They knew He had special favor with God. We are told, "Jesus grew in wisdom and stature, and in favor with God and man" (Luke 2:52).

When Lazarus died, "Martha said to Jesus, 'if you had been here, my brother would not have died. But I know that even now God will give you whatever you ask.' Jesus said to her, 'Your brother will rise again' " (John 11:21-23).

Martha and Mary had been hosting and caring for Jesus in their home for free. Even Mary had gone to the extent of wiping His feet with her hair and precious ointment.

When Lazarus died they leveraged on the favor they had with Jesus and sent a "WhatsApp" message to Him, asking Him to interrupt His busy schedule and come and raise Lazarus from the dead.

Jesus came, and when they got to the tomb, Jesus said, " 'Take away the stone.'

'But, Lord,' said Martha, the sister of the dead man, 'by this time there is a bad odor, for he has been there four days.'

Then Jesus said, 'Did I not tell you that if you believe, you will see the glory of God?'

So they took away the stone. Then Jesus looked up and said, 'Father, I thank you that you have heard me. I knew that you always hear me, but I said this for the benefit of the people standing here, that they may believe that you sent me.'

When he had said this, Jesus called in a loud voice, 'Lazarus, come out!' The dead man came out, his hands and feet wrapped with strips of linen, and a cloth around his face.

Jesus said to them, 'Take off the grave clothes and let him go' " (John 11:39-44).

Their spiritual account was pregnant with favor. They were able to draw on the intangible power of God and bring their brother back to life.

Favor Can "Buy" a Spouse

She was a simple, orphaned, second-class citizen because she was a descendant of slaves. She was the cousin of Mordecai, a man who worked as security detail at the gate of the king's palace. Mordecai became his adopted father because of their age gap.

Who would have thought that this simple girl from a very humble background could rise to become queen? How could someone from such a low social, political, and economic background rise to such a level? Miraculously she became the queen of the most powerful empire at that time. Her name was Esther. How did the impossible become possible? She found favor in the eye of the king.

A beauty pageant was organized for the king to select a wife. When all the lovely girls were paraded, "the king was attracted to Esther more than to any of the other women, and she won his favor and approval more than any of the other virgins. So he set a royal crown on her head and made her queen instead of Vashti" (Esther 2:17).

You can't buy that with money. That's why favor is a superior currency. Although Esther did not serve the king, the point here is to establish the power of favor.

Favor can buy you a marriage made in heaven.

Favor Can "Buy" the Anointing

I have been serving my pastor, Dag Heward-Mills, for many years, and I believe this service has opened doors of favor to me spiritually and naturally. One of the things I have received through him is the anointing, or the power of God. I have had different visions where God has used him to offer me many things, from the power of God, to a large congregation, to money. Favor has transferred some of the anointing he carries upon my life. It reminded me of how Elisha became anointed.

Elijah said to Elisha, " 'Tell me, what can I do for you before I am taken from you?'

'Let me inherit a double portion of your spirit,' Elisha replied.

'You have asked a difficult thing,' Elijah said, 'yet if you see me when I am taken from you, it will be yours—otherwise, it will not.'

As they were walking along and talking together, suddenly a chariot of fire and horses of fire appeared and separated the two of them, and Elijah went up to heaven in a whirlwind" (2 Kings 2:9-11).

Favor Can Protect You

I once read a story about a journalist who was captured by rebels in Congo, where he had gone to cover a story. When the rebels brought him to their camp, the journalist greeted the rebel leader in their local language. He was surprised that a white man could speak the local dialect.

He asked him where he learnt the language from. He explained that his mother used to be a missionary in Congo when he was young, so he lived there for some years. The rebel leader asked, "Is you mother Mrs. So-and-so?"

He replied, "Yes."

Suddenly the man beamed with smiles, and mentioned the mother's name. He said, "That woman immunized me and taught me in Sunday school."

Because of this the journalist was released and given an interview. Her mother's free labor of love to save the life of that young boy years before saved the life of her own son.

Favor in this story was obtained through free service. "Surely, LORD, you bless the righteous; you surround them with your favor as with a shield" (Psalm 5:12).

Favor Can Release Resources

The Example of Nehemiah
Nehemiah was a slave boy who served the king of Babylon, Ahasareus, for many years.
One day the king noticed that the countenance of Nehemiah had fallen. When he inquired, Nehemiah told him about the walls of Jerusalem, which were broken down, and his desire to rebuild the walls. He said to the king, "If it pleases the king and if your servant has found favor in his sight, let him send me to the city in Judah where my ancestors are buried so that I can rebuild it" (Nehemiah 2:5).

Because of the favor he had acquired through his free service, the king assisted him with resources to rebuild the walls of Jerusalem. This favor came by working for free.

Favor Can Increase or Decrease

Because favor is a currency, it can increase or decrease in quantity, like any currency. Service to others will increase the level of favor on your life, especially if it's voluntary, because people will feel they owe you something.

Favor can be increased intentionally. Jesus increased the level of favor on His life, and so can you. "Jesus grew in wisdom and stature, and in favor with God and man" (Luke 2:52).

Favor can also decrease through disservice, the opposite of service.

In the book of Esther, Vashti, the queen, lost favor and her position because of her bad attitude. A bad attitude will always deplete your "favor account."

Disfavor can create a hostile marriage, and deplete the favor that some children have with their parents. Disfavor can cause you to lose your job. Favor can be depleted and move into negative territory.

The Story of Vashti

There was a queen named Vashti, the wife of a powerful king who reigned over a vast empire. The king organized a great banquet and asked his servants "to bring before him Queen Vashti, wearing her royal crown, in order to display her beauty to the people and nobles, for she was lovely to look at. But when the attendants delivered the king's command, Queen Vashti refused to come. Then the king became furious and burned with anger" (Esther 1:11-12).

Suddenly the favor she enjoyed was discounted, like a Black Friday sale. This was the decision taken concerning her by the king: "Vashti is never again to enter the presence of King Xerxes. Also let the king give her royal position to someone else who is better than she" (Esther 1:19). Favor can increase or decrease, based on what you do.

You can deliberately grow favor by working for free. "And Jesus grew in wisdom and stature, and in favor with God and man" (Luke 2:52). He ministered for free. For example, He did not charge when He raised Lazarus from the dead.

3. Profit Has to Be Identified: Relationships

How I Met My Wife

When I was in the university, I was a very serious Christian and I led many people to Christ. I had a friend called Naakai who initially did not know the Lord. I spoke to her about Jesus and she gave her life to Him. I taught her how to pray and helped her to grow in the Lord. All my labour "seemed" to be for free, because the Lord never paid me physically for my efforts.

One day we were having coffee together when I saw a beautiful Christian girl I knew on campus approaching us. I knew her from afar, but I had never spoken to her before. I was excited, because a dream was walking into my reality. A question that had been on my heart for a long time, from the time I was born, was about to be answered. The question was, "Who is my better half?" On that day I saw the answer to the question walking towards me.

She introduced herself as Adwoa. We started chatting and we became friends on that day. The womb of time later delivered my wife to me. I had been working for the Lord for free and I got a wonderful wife as my pay. We have been married for twenty-five years and our relationship has been excellent. Out of this relationship we have four beautiful children: two boys and two girls.

One of the greatest gifts God can give you is a godly, wonderful spouse. "Houses and wealth are inherited from parents, but a prudent wife is from the LORD" (Proverbs 19:14).

Sometime your profit for your labour is not money, but a spouse or vital relationships. What can be better than that?

Faithful Paul

I once had a faithful and good gentleman called Paul work for me for free for some time. I was so touched. I opened national and international doors for him. Through me he came to know the Lord because he was originally a Muslim. He is now a good husband, father, and Christian. He is a blessed man, and it started when he worked for me for free.

People produce money; money does not produce people. That's why people are more valuable than money. Abraham once rescued the king of Sodom from captivity. This king offered to pay him. The king of Sodom said to Abram, "Give me the people and keep the goods for yourself." He was a smart man who he knew the value of relationships (Genesis 14:21).

4. Profit Has to Be Identified: Experience

My Building Experience

My father once said to me, "Experience is the best teacher, only the school fees can be very high." There is an African proverb that states, "The old man sitting under the Iroko tree can see further than the young man standing on top of the tree." The Bible seems to support this statement. Jesus said: "Anyone who sets aside one of the least of these commands and teaches others accordingly will be called least in the kingdom of heaven, but whoever practices and teaches these commands will be called great in the kingdom of heaven" (Matthew 5:19).

The best teachers are those who have experienced what they are teaching. The profit you make for working for free can be valuable experience.

My Father

My father was a real estate developer, and when I was young he often took me to the building site to work. I really detested it because it was hard and he never paid me for it. He used to say, "I am training you," but I used to think he was just a hard man. Through that I gained a lot of practical building experience very early in life. That was one of the things that inspired me to study architecture.

I learnt about leadership, negotiation, empathy, human nature, discipline, and how to interact with different people. All these experiences have shaped my life, and currently as a pastor I have been directly involved in the building of at least over fifty church buildings locally and internationally. Apart from that, I have managed multimillion-dollar building projects. I am still making profit from that experience.

Marital Experience

It takes experience to succeed at anything, including marriage.

As a pastor I sometimes come across women who want to marry, but no one seems to be approaching them. This can be caused by inexperience in relating to the opposite sex. Some people know how to press the right buttons, and before you are aware, you will be standing at the altar, saying marital vows.

The Story of Ruth

In the Bible there is a Moabite woman called Ruth. The name of her mother-in-law was Naomi. When her husband and kids died, Naomi decided to return to her home country, Israel.

Ruth decided to follow her mother-in-law and serve her because she had lost her husband. Ruth said to Naomi, " 'Don't urge me to leave you or to turn back from you. Where you go I will go, and where you stay I will stay. Your people will be my people and your God my God. Where you die I will die, and there I will be buried. May the Lord deal with me, be it ever so severely, if even death separates you and me' " (Ruth 1:16-17). When Naomi realized that Ruth was determined to go with her, she stopped discouraging her.

On the surface it looks like Naomi has nothing to offer Ruth because she was old and a widow. What she had was experience. "The glory of young men is their strength, gray hair the splendor of the old" (Proverbs 20:29). When you grow old, your strength shifts from muscle to experience.

An Experienced Person Can Coach You to Marry

Naomi, the older lady, coached Ruth to remarry. She married a rich, godly man called Boaz. What I find interesting about Naomi's coaching is, it was a mixture of legal, spiritual, and natural principles.

Legally there was a law in Israel at that time that the nearest relative of a deceased husband could marry the surviving widow. Ruth did not understand the customs of her new country, so she was schooled by Naomi. She also taught her how to catch Boaz' attention, because there were other interested young girls.

She advised her to go and apply for work in Boaz' field and not to take a break during break so she would stand out and be noticed. It worked, because she stuck out like a beautiful flower; Boaz noticed her.

Naomi also taught Ruth how to look presentable and attractive. Naomi said to Ruth, " 'Wash, put on perfume, and get dressed in your best clothes. Then go down to the threshing floor, but don't let him know you are there until he has finished eating and drinking' " (Ruth 3:3).

She also coached her about timing. She told her to approach him after he had finished eating and drinking. Naturally he would be relaxed and in a good mood.

When you propose love to someone, make sure your location and timing is right. There is "a time to love and a time to hate, a time for war and a time for peace" (Ecclesiastes 3:8). I had a friend who proposed to someone in a taxi. He was bounced like a ball. The setting was wrong.

Spiritually I believe she went into serious prayer. "Naomi said to Ruth, 'Wait, my daughter, until you find out what happens. For the man will not rest until the matter is settled today' " (Ruth 3:18). She said, "Until he marries you, he will never be at peace."

Is there a delay in your marriage? Are you hearing excuses? If it's God's will that the person should marry you, may he or she not know peace till it's done. "So Boaz took Ruth and she became his wife. When he made love to her, the LORD enabled her to conceive, and she gave birth to a son.... The women living there said, 'Naomi has a son!' And they named him Obed. He was the father of Jesse, the father of David" (Ruth 4:13, 17).

Chapter 4

What to Do after Identifying Your "Profit"

1. What to Do after Identifying Your Profit: Use Your Profit As Leverage

The Flat Tire

SOMETIME BACK a friend of mine and I had a flat tire on an uneven road. When we tried to jack the car, we discovered the tire could not be suspended high enough for us to remove it. We found a long piece of metal and placed it under the car. With it we were able to raise the car a little bit more and change the tire. The bar acted as a lever.

Leverage is the ability to use something as an advantage to achieve a desired result. Just as we used the bar as leverage to raise the car, you can also use the "profit" you have made by working for free as a lever to achieve your desired result. Skill, favor, relationships, etc., can all be used as a lever to obtain a desired result.

Knowledge Can Be Used As Leverage

You can leverage on someone's marital experience. I have a friend who grew up with a single mom. One thing I observed was she did not know how to interact well with her husband. She was disrespectful and rude and I came to the conclusion it was because she had not seen married people interacting before.

She struggled in marriage and eventually divorced. Had she intentionally learned the skills of marriage from a successful couple, she could have leveraged on her acquired skill to have a successful marriage.

Assuming you were not married and you were friends with a successful marriage, you could volunteer to babysit their child. This will give you the opportunity to learn practical marital skills from them. When you marry, you can use the knowledge you have gained as leverage to have a successful marriage.

Sometimes when you have not seen something before, it's difficult to duplicate it.

Experience Can Be Used As Leverage

Younger people can use the experience of older people as leverage. Paul told Pastor Timothy he expected the younger women to learn from the older ones. He said, "Likewise, teach the older women to be reverent in the way they live, not to be slanderers or addicted to much wine, but to teach what is good. Then they can urge the younger women to love their husbands and children" (Titus 2:3-4).

It's amazing that even love has to be learnt. Love is not just an emotion; it's also seen in your actions. It's possible to be in love emotionally and be out of love physically. The older, married women were supposed to teach the younger how to communicate love in action. Sometimes the actions of well-intended people who claim they love you can rather kill your marriage. This is a skill that can be learnt.

A Skill Can Be Used As Leverage

David Used a Catapult As Leverage

Take the story of David. He learnt the skill of throwing stones while working for his dad for free as a shepherd. He developed the skill so much he used it to kill lions and bears. One day there was a fight with the Philistines. "And there went out a champion out of the camp of the Philistines, named Goliath, of Gath, whose height was six cubits and a span. And he had an helmet of brass upon his head, and he was armed with a coat of mail; and the weight of the coat was five thousand shekels of brass" (1 Samuel 17:4-5, KJV). Goliath was about ten feet tall, about the height of a three-story building. What a formidable enemy.

David leveraged on his skill of throwing stones. Leverage, as I explained earlier, is the ability to use something as an advantage to achieve a desired result. "He took his staff in his hand, chose five smooth stones from the stream, put them in the pouch of his shepherd's bag and, with his sling in his hand, approached the Philistine.... As the Philistine moved closer to attack him, David ran quickly toward the battle line to meet him. Reaching into his bag and taking out a stone, he slung it and struck the Philistine on the forehead. The stone sank into his forehead, and he fell face-down on the ground. So David triumphed over the Philistine with a sling and a stone; without a sword in his hand he struck down the Philistine and killed him" (1 Samuel 17:40, 48-50).

David used his catapult as a lever to claim the price of wealth, marriage, and exemption from paying taxes. Before the battle, the men of Israel said to him, "Do you see how this man keeps coming out? He comes out to defy Israel. The king will give great wealth to the man who kills him. He will also give him his daughter in marriage and will exempt his family from taxes in Israel" (1 Samuel 17:25).

Under normal circumstances, David could not have married the daughter of a king because of his social and financial status. In his own self-admission, he said, "Do you think it is a small matter to become the king's son-in-law? I'm only a poor man and little known" (1 Samuel 18:23).

When you leverage on your skill, you will be surprised the kind of girl you will marry; a girl behind your dreams. A man who marries the daughter of a wealthy man said, "It's not only women who can marry into wealth; men can also marry into wealth."

I want to encourage spiritual young men who don't have money but are competing for the same girl with an unbeliever. Don't leverage on money, because you will be outspent and you will become broke. Leverage on your skills. You have the anointing and can speak in tongues. Begin to pray in an unknown tongue: "Ras kata kata kata." Leverage on your skill and claim the love of your life.

Identify your profit, be it the anointing, experience, exposure, education, a skill, favor, or something you learnt from someone. Use it as a lever to achieve your desired results.

2. What to Do after Identifying Your Profit: Utilize It

What I Learnt from My Dad

To utilize means to use what you have. Just yesterday I was having a conversation with my son and I told him one thing I learnt from my dad. My dad did not believe in debt or loans. I have utilized this knowledge to my advantage. By God's grace I am debt free and hope to remain so. When I pay for stuff I use my debit card or pay cash. I only use a credit card for airline tickets or hotels because I have no choice, but I make sure I pay it off immediately. I am utilizing the wisdom I learnt from my dad.

I said to my son, "People sometimes pile up debts because they want to own things they cannot afford." I continued, "Utilize what you have also learnt from me. Don't own things you cannot afford and live within your means." It may sound old-school, but being in debt is not encouraged in the Bible. It has many negative connotations.

The Pastor Who Failed to Utilize What He Had Learnt

There was this pastor who worked under a great man of God for many years. One day he left to start his own ministry. I was surprised to learn he was doing the opposite of all that he had learnt. His ministry did not prosper.

He did not utilize the skills he had learnt while serving this man. It's possible to learn from anointed people and not utilize what you learnt.

The Example of Paul

The great apostle Paul had a protégé called Timothy. This young man served him in the ministry. When he started pastoring his own church, Paul urged him to utilize all he had learnt from him. He said to him, "You, however, know all about my teaching, my way of life, my purpose, faith, patience, love, endurance, persecutions, sufferings — what kinds of things happened to me in Antioch, Iconium and Lystra, the persecutions I endured. Yet the Lord rescued me from all of

them.... But as for you, continue in what you have learned and have become convinced of, because you know those from whom you learned it" (2 Timothy 3:10-1, 3:14).
Timothy served Paul in ministry and Paul expected him to utilize what he had learnt from him. One of the things Timothy could utilize was Paul's "way of life." He had been close enough to see how Paul prayed, conducted meetings, how he spent his time, the food he ate, how long he slept, how he related to the opposite sex, etc.

The Example of the Prodigal Son
Sometimes you can come across children of wealthy parents who grow up to be paupers. Although they lived with wealthy people, they did not learn anything or refused to utilize what they had learnt.

The prodigal son is a good example. When he was in his father's house he did everything right, but the minute he left home he decided not to utilize all he had learnt. This is his story. "There was a man who had two sons. The younger one said to his father, 'Father, give me my share of the estate.' So he divided his property between them. Not long after that, the younger son got together all he had, set off for a distant country and there squandered his wealth in wild living. After he had spent everything, there was a severe famine in that whole country, and he began to be in need" (Luke 15:11-14).

His father was a rich, hardworking, righteous man. He did not have a lavish lifestyle, nor hook up with prostitutes, but this boy did not utilize all these values. He lost all his inheritance. Let me ask you a question. What good virtue have you learnt that you have refused to utilize?

3. What to Do after Identifying Your Profit: Monetize It

To monetize means to convert something into money. To make financial gain out of skills you have learnt by working for free you must be able to monetize it.

David converted his skill at throwing stones into money. As a skill it was not of much use to him till he decided to monetize it. David did not fight Goliath because he wanted to save Israel; he fought him because of the prize money. Before lifting a finger, "David asked the men standing by him, 'What will be done for the man who kills this Philistine and removes this disgrace from Israel? Who is this uncircumcised Philistine that he should defy the armies of the living God?' They repeated to him what they had been saying and told him, 'This is what will be done for the man who kills him.' " (1 Samuel 17:26-27). He was informed the prize was money, a beautiful girl, and exemption from paying taxes.

The fact that you have acquired a skill does not mean it will be of benefit to you. Monetize it. Colonel Sanders, the founder of KFC was a good cook. When he realized his fried chicken recipe was celebrated, he monetized it, and that gave birth to the multibillion-dollar KFC franchise.

Chapter 5

How You Can Profit from Serving the Lord

WHEN YOU SERVE the Lord you can profit naturally and in spiritual ways. Let's begin by looking at some examples.

Natural Profit

1. How You Can Profit from Serving the Lord: Public Speaking Skills
My twin brother is a lawyer and a lay pastor. He is the senior pastor of a church and has a congregation. He is not paid for pastoring because it's a voluntary job. However, he profits in many ways from serving the Lord for free.

One day his boss was supposed to do a presentation but he couldn't, so he asked him to do it. After his presentation his boss was wowed. He asked him if he had been trained as a professional speaker. He was surprised at his eloquence, delivery, and confidence. What his boss did not know was that he was drawing from his skill as a pastor. Because of this, he does a lot of presentations and has risen in his role due to this and several factors.

I have noticed that when you volunteer to serve in the church, it also helps you to develop leadership skills.

2. How You Can Profit from Serving the Lord: Leadership Skills

It's more difficult to organize people voluntarily than when you pay them. When you pay them, the risk of firing makes people more compliant. When you don't, you will need to use pure leadership skills to lead them.

For example, when you are the leader of a choir you will have to learn to manage different personalities over a wider spectrum. You will have to manage millionaires and the poor, the old and the young, the educated and not so educated, etc.

3. How You Can Profit from Serving the Lord: Networking

Networking is making an effort to meet new people who may be beneficial to you.

A church is a great place for networking. It gives you a diverse group of people to relate to. Most of our relationships are homogenous. In a legal office, everyone is likely to be a lawyer or related to law. In an architectural office, everyone will have something to do with buildings.

Serving the Lord will make you come into contact with diverse people. Look at what the Bible says about spiritual networking in a church: "And not holding the Head, from which all the body by joints and bands having nourishment ministered, and knit together, increaseth with the increase of God" (Colossians 2:19, KJV).

In summary, we are to maintain our connection with the Head, Christ, and other members of the body of Christ. The result is we will be nourished spiritually. To nourish means to supply with what is necessary. The result is growth. It could be marital relationships, a job, or even advice.

Assuming you take up a counseling role in the church, you may come into contact with people who are outside your normal scope. As a pastor, I have met millionaires, thieves, CEOs, children, wizards, politicians, name it. Through some of these interactions I have made some serious beneficial relationships.

Let's take an example of the church at Antioch. "Now in the church at Antioch there were prophets and teachers: Barnabas, Simeon called Niger, Lucius of Cyrene, Manaen (who had been brought up with Herod the tetrarch) and Saul" (Acts 13:1).

Take the example of the church at Antioch. Manaen was politically connected because he hand been brought up with Herod the Tetrach, who ruled in Galilee. Herod was the official title and Tetrach means "ruler of a quarter."

Spiritual Profit

1. How You Can Profit from Serving the Lord: Peace

The most precious things in life are invisible. The human body itself is a metaphor of this truth. We give so much attention to our lips, hair, nails eyebrows, and clothes.

It's ironic that the most important parts of the body are invisible to the eye. I have never heard someone being praised for having a beautiful kidney or heart, but I have heard people being praised for having nice eyes. You can survive without eyes, but you cannot survive without a heart.

The Wedding Reception

I have a nephew called Joshua. I was asked to say something at his wedding and give him a piece of advice. I said, "Joshua, a happy marriage is an atmosphere of love, peace, and joy. It does not matter if you live in a mansion or have a full bank account. If you do not have this intangible blessing you will not enjoy marriage, irrespective of what you have."

Scripture supports this statement. It says it is "better to live on a corner of the roof than share a house with a quarrelsome wife.... It is better to live in a desert than with a quarrelsome and nagging wife" (Proverbs 21:9, 19).

Peace has no price. It's one of the greatest gifts God can give to you. No wonder one of the last gifts of Jesus to His disciples who had been serving Him was peace. He said, "Peace I leave with you; my peace I give you. I do not give to you as the world gives. Do not let your hearts be troubled and do not be afraid" (John 14:27).

2. How You Can Profit from Serving the Lord: Eternal Rewards

One day a friend of mine came to visit me with his kids. Finally, when they were leaving, his kids took some of my kids' toys into their car. Their father took away the toys from them and told them they were not theirs but had only been lent to them for a while.

The toys of this world: the cars, buildings, etc., are not ours. They have only been lent to us by God to play with for a while. We cannot take them away when we die. We must leave them behind.

Not everything in life has eternal value. Most things are precious in time but became useless in death. Natural speaking, many currencies lose their value as soon as you cross borders. That's why things become valueless when you cross the border of death.

The only thing of eternal value is what you have done for God. For most people this will be voluntary. You serve God by preaching, visiting, witnessing, praying, etc. This is what John heard when he went to heaven: "Then I heard a voice from heaven say, 'Write this: Blessed are the dead who die in the Lord from now on.' 'Yes,' says the Spirit, 'they will rest from their labor, for their deeds will follow them' " (Revelation 14:13-14).

Your job, car, house, or money can't follow you, but your labor in the Lord can follow. These works will bring you eternal rewards.

3. How You Can Profit from Serving the Lord: Grace

Serving the Lord makes you access the grace of God. I have been serving the Lord for over thirty years, and sometimes it looked like my labor was in vain.

When you work for God it can look unprofitable because you don't receive a physical cheque from heaven saying, "We are paying you fifty dollars for visiting Sister Mary when she was sick." Because of this, many people think it's unprofitable to win souls, visit the sick, and care for people. You may even have to use your own money while doing that.

My Experience

I had been living and pastoring in a certain city for many years. I started ministry as a student and pastor at the same time. I had to work hard and long to make this possible. I did not receive cheques from heaven.

One day I was transferred by my church, so I had to leave everything I had worked for behind and move with my wife, who had a medical practice in that city. It exerted a great financial toll on us. It was like I was beginning life all over again. It seemed to me my life had been reversed at least ten years backwards because my circumstances looked like where I was ten years earlier.

We moved into a smaller house, which was uncomfortable, and I remember my wife asking me if I was going to build a new house. I answered no because I think I was sad, sad because I had lost the church I had built for many years and my house. I had lost vision and energy, but God saved me.

There are times when God demonstrates His grace towards us with supernatural signs and wonders.

The Visitation of Jesus

One night I was asleep when I felt someone tapping me. I thought it was my wife, but when I opened my eyes I saw Jesus standing in the room. I said, "Jesus!" I could not believe it. He smiled at me and said, "I have been listening to your conversation with your wife and I heard you say you were not going to build another house." There is a Scripture that says God listens to the conversations of those who fear Him. It's says, "Then those who feared the LORD talked with each other, and the LORD listened and heard. A scroll of remembrance was written in his presence concerning those who feared the LORD and honored his name" (Malachi 3:16).

That day that Scripture became real to me. He continued, "I am going to build a better and a brand new house for you in ten months."

I answered, "Lord, I don't have money even to buy land, and I cannot build a whole house in ten months."

He said. "I will build it, not you, and it will be built debt free. In addition, I will build a brand new five-thousand-seat church auditorium in two years. This will also be debt free," He added.

I protested, "There are only about two hundred people in the church, and most of them are not rich. They can't build it."

He said, "That's why I am going to do it." He said, "I will supply the money. This will also be debt free."

I was bewildered and confused. I did not know how all this could be done within such a short frame of time. God's power is usually manifested in our weakness.

He once said to the apostle Paul, " 'My grace is sufficient for you, for my power is made perfect in weakness.' Therefore I will boast all the more gladly about my weaknesses, so that Christ's power may rest on me. That is why, for Christ's sake, I delight in weaknesses, in insults, in hardships, in persecutions, in difficulties. For when I am weak, then I am strong" (2 Corinthians 12:9-10).

In the morning I told my wife about the visitation of Jesus and what He said to me.

Through a series of strange events that started unfolding within twenty-four hours, both prophecies came to pass within the stipulated time. The house was built in nine months and the church was finished within twenty months. That church is now full to overflowing.

Friend, don't think that your labor in the Lord is for free. If that labor is expended under the right conditions, you will reap tangible and intangible blessings.

4. How You Can Profit from Serving the Lord: Eternal Life

When I was in my teens, I fell ill one day and had a near-death experience. One night as I lay on my bed I saw my spirit come out of my body. I could see myself looking at my physical body. There was this dark, shadowy figure in human form standing by my side.

He caught me by the hand in a vicelike grip. The ground opened to reveal a tunnel, which descended into the earth. We descended down this dark shaft and I wondered where we were going. The tunnel started getting warmer, and at one point I could hear people screaming. The screams started getting louder till I saw this huge fire in the distance. I knew

I was destined for hell. I begin to cry out to Jesus and a voice boomed in the tunnel. It said, "Leave that boy alone let's give him another chance." The evil spirit released its grip and I saw myself flying through the tunnel and into my bedroom. My spirit dived into my body and I came back to life.

The ultimate profit you can make in life is to have eternal life by knowing Jesus as your savior and Lord.

That experience showed me the horror of hell. Not long after I became born again and gave my life to Jesus. I now enjoy the gift of eternal life and will meet Jesus when I die.

The story of Lazarus and the rich man throws biblical light on this subject. "There was a rich man who was dressed in purple and fine linen and lived in luxury every day. At his gate was laid a beggar named Lazarus, covered with sores and longing to eat what fell from the rich man's table. Even the dogs came and licked his sores.

"The time came when the beggar died and the angels carried him to Abraham's side. The rich man also died and was buried. In Hades, where he was in torment, he looked up and saw Abraham far away, with Lazarus by his side. So he called to him, 'Father Abraham, have pity on me and send Lazarus to dip the tip of his finger in water and cool my tongue, because I am in agony in this fire.'

"But Abraham replied, 'Son, remember that in your lifetime you received your good things, while Lazarus received bad things, but now he is comforted here and you are in agony. And besides all this, between us and you a great chasm has been set in place, so that those who want to go from here to you cannot, nor can anyone cross over from there to us' " (Luke 16:19-26).

Death Is Not the End of Life

It is said that nothing is lost in the universe; it only changes form. For example, water is a liquid but it can change into a solid form and become an ice cube when frozen. It can also change into a gas when you boil it.

When we die, we only change from physical beings to spirit beings and we continue living. Death is not the end of life; it's the beginning of another life.

There is profit in free labor. May God grant you understanding to maximize your profits.

If you don't know the Lord Jesus and you want to be saved and serve Him, I can help you do that. First of all, you need to repent of your sins. Secondly, pray this prayer after me.

> Lord Jesus, I repent of my sins and I believe that You died for me. Wash away my sins with Your blood, the only spiritual detergent for sin, and make me Your child.

I encourage you to find a good Bible-believing church to attend. Don't forget to profit from free labor. God bless you.

Chapter 6

Conditions for Serving God

GOD'S PROMISES are conditional, and to profit from serving the Lord, you must do it under the right conditions. What are some of the conditions?

1. Conditions for Serving God: Don't Be Cynical

Serving God is profitable. Don't join carnal people who think it's unprofitable. In the days of Malachi, some people viewed service to God as useless. This was God's response to them.

" 'You have spoken arrogantly against me,' says the Lord.

'Yet you ask, "What have we said against you?"

'You have said, "It is futile to serve God. What do we gain by carrying out his requirements and going about like mourners before the Lord Almighty? But now we call the arrogant blessed. Certainly evildoers prosper, and even when they put God to the test, they get away with it." '

"Then those who feared the Lord talked with each other, and the Lord listened and heard. A scroll of remembrance was written in his presence concerning those who feared the Lord and honored his name.

'On the day when I act,' says the LORD Almighty, 'they will be my treasured possession. I will spare them, just as a father has compassion and spares his son who serves him. And you will again see the distinction between the righteous and the wicked, between those who serve God and those who do not' " (Malachi 3:13-18).

Deliverance from evil is one of the benefits of serving God.

2. Conditions for Serving God: You Must Work for the Lord

"For God is not unrighteous to forget your work and labour of love, which ye have shewed toward his name, in that ye have ministered to the saints, and do minister" (Hebrews 6:10, KJV). This means you must involve yourself in the work of God. Either as a lay person or a pastor.

The church of God provides a context for you to serve God. You may be a gifted footballer but you still need a team. Join the choir, the children's church, witness, visit, pray, by all means, do something.

3. Conditions for Serving God: You Must Do Everything in the Name of Jesus

This means whatever you do must be for His glory, not yours. Paul said to the church of Corinth, "So whether you eat or drink or whatever you do, do it all for the glory of God" (1 Corinthians 10:31).

4. Conditions for Serving God: Your Labor Must Be a Labor of Love

This refers to your motivation. You must work out of love for God and not love for anything else. The Bible calls it the royal law. It encapsulates all you can do for God. "For God is not unrighteous to forget your work and labour of love" (Hebrews 6:10, KJV).

Conclusion

There is profit in free labor. To make profit you must redefine your definition of profit, identify the profit you seek. Leverage, monetize, and utilize your profit, and finally, may you enjoy the cryptocurrency called "free labor."

About the Author
Kakra Baiden

MANY YEARS AGO the Lord Jesus Christ appeared in a vision to Kakra Baiden and called him into the ministry as a prophet, teacher, and miracle worker. He is also known as "the walking Bible" for his supernatural ability to preach and teach the Bible from memory.

Pastor Baiden is an architect by profession and serves as a bishop of the Lighthouse Chapel International denomination. He has trained many pastors and planted many churches within the Lighthouse denomination.

Currently he is the senior pastor of the Morning Star Cathedral, Lighthouse Chapel International, Accra. He is a sought-after revivalist and conference speaker.

He is also the president of Airpower, a ministry through which he touches the world through radio and TV broadcasts, books, CDs, videos, the Internet, and international conferences dubbed "The Airpower Conference." He has ministered the Word on every continent and is also the author of the best-selling book, *Squatters*.

Pastor Baiden is married to Lady Rev. Dr. Ewuradwoa Baiden and they have four children.

For additional information on Kakra Baiden's books and messages (CDs and DVDs), write to any of these addresses:

US
26219 Halbrook Glen Lane
Katy, TX 77494

UK
32 Tern Road
Hampton, Hargate
Cambridgeshire
Pe78DG

GHANA
P.O. Box SK 1067
Sakumono Estates, Tema
Ghana-West Africa

E-MAIL: info@kakrabaiden.org
WEBSITE: www.kakrabaiden.org
FACEBOOK: www.facebook.com/KakraBaiden
TWITTER: www.twitter.com/ProphetKakraB

CPSIA information can be obtained
at www.ICGtesting.com
Printed in the USA
LVHW051117120419
613962LV00001B/1

9 781945 123177